Donald Trump!
Yearbook

ALWAYS 100% UNOFFICIAL

Adam G Goodwin
Jonathan Parkyn

PORTICO

Donald Trump!
Yearbook

First published in the United Kingdom in 2019 by

Portico
43 Great Ormond Street
London
WC1N 3HZ

An imprint of Pavilion Books Company Ltd
Copyright © Pavilion Books Company Ltd 2019
Text copyright © Yes/No Publishing Services 2019

ISBN 978-1-91162-232-1

A CIP catalogue record for this book is available from the British Library.

10 9 8 7 6 5 4 3 2 1

Reproduction by Rival Colour Ltd, UK
Printed and bound by Elcograf, Italy

This book can be ordered direct from the publisher at
www.pavilionbooks.com

THIS BOOK BELONGS TO

_____

Contents!

Contents!

Welcome!

Hey, Everyone!

Welcome to the first ever and totally 100% Unofficial Donald Trump Yearbook! Donald loves hamburgers, and if this book were a burger then it would be the most deliciously lip-smacking burger you ever ate! In fact we have cooked up such an irresistibly yummy book for you we almost ate the whole damn thing ourselves! Not literally of course, that would be crazy!!:-)

Inside Donald's own yearbook you will find a veritable feast of delectable delights to gorge on. Spot the naughty 'Trumpkins' in the Great Trump Clone Hunt Game, make your ultimate president with Mr. Potus Head, chillax on the beach with the Trump Cabana Tropical Banana Word Search and be at one with yourself with the Magical Joy of Trumpfulness. With poster pics, puzzles, fun masks, games, quizzes and questionnaires, along with the enchanting 'Chronicles of Mel-narnia' and the enterprising 'Trump Trek' short stories for dessert, this is one banquet of a book that you will savour forever!

Bon Appetit!

The Editor

PRESIDENTIAL SMACKDOWN CARDS

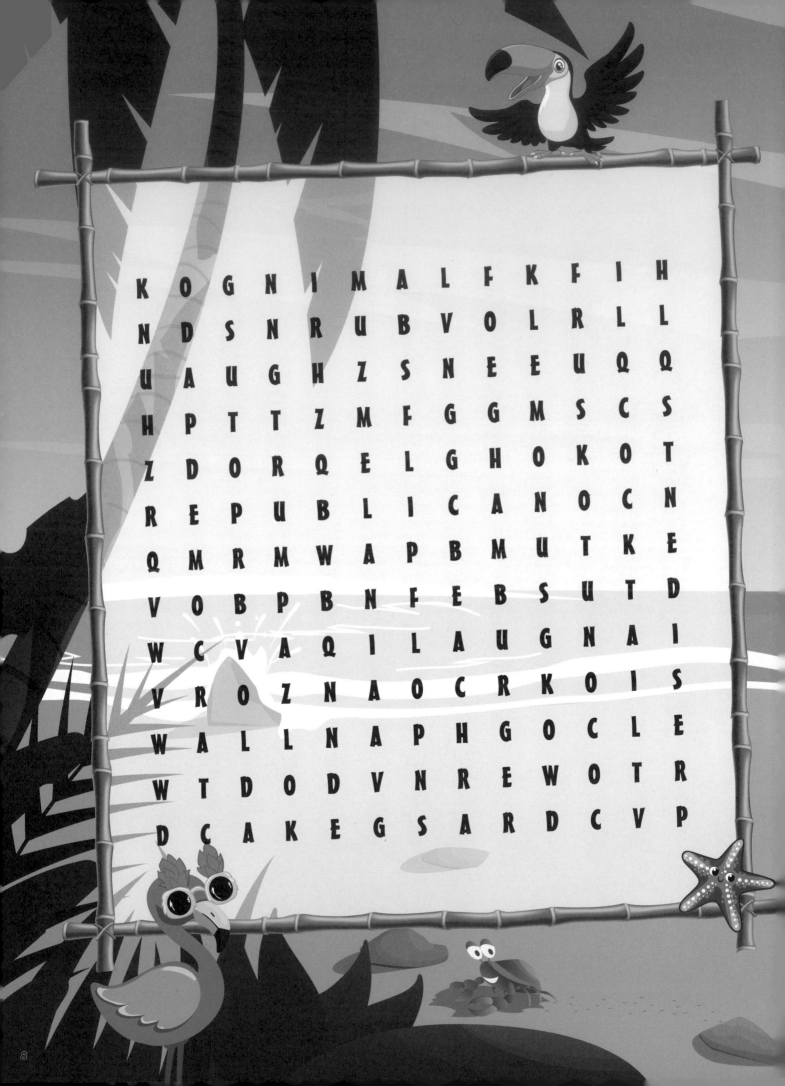

```
K O G N I M A L F K F I H
N D S N R U B V O L R L L
U A U G H Z S N E E U Q Q
H P T T Z M F G G M S C S
Z D O R Q E L G H O K O T
R E P U B L I C A N O C N
Q M R M W A P B M U T K E
V O B P B N F E B S U T D
W C V A Q I L A U G N A I
V R O Z N A O C R K O I S
W A L L N A P H G O C L E
W T D O D V N R E W O T R
D C A K E G S A R D C V P
```

TRUMP CABANA TROPICAL BANANA BEACH VACATION WORD SEARCH

Even presidents need a vacation!

Why not join Donald at his favourite retreat, kick back with a Mojito and complete this tropical, presidential, Trump-related word search.

REPUBLICAN	COCONUT	DEMOCRAT
QUEENS	SUN	FLAMINGO
BEACH	FLIPFLOP	PRESIDENT
TAN	TOWER	COCKTAIL
SURF	TRUMP	BURN
MELANIA	CAKE	HAMBURGER
POTUS	BANANA WALL	LEMON

39 JIMMY 'PEANUTS' CARTER

CATCHPHRASE: "Eat my nuts!"

PHYSICAL STRENGTH:

NEMESIS: Ted "Frenemy" Kennedy

SIGNATURE MOVE: The P'Nutcracker

APOCALYPSE RATING:

WORLD WRESTLING PRESIDENTS

40 **RONNIE "THE RAY GUN" REAGAN**

CATCHPHRASE: "I ain't monkeying around!"

PHYSICAL STRENGTH:

NEMESIS: Leapin' Leonid Brezhnev

SIGNATURE MOVE: The Slick-back Dragon Whip

APOCALYPSE RATING:

WORLD WRESTLING PRESIDENTS

DONALD'S 'EXCITING' ELECTION EXPERIENCE COLOURING-IN GAME

STATES CAN SWING FROM RED TO BLUE (& VICE VERSA) AT THE ROLL OF A DICE!

LET LUCKY 'LADY CHANCE' DECIDE YOUR PRESIDENTIAL FATE!

HAVE YOU EVER DREAMED OF BEING A PRESIDENTIAL CANDIDATE ON ELECTION NIGHT? WHO HASN'T? WELL, NOW YOU CAN EXPERIENCE ALL THE HIGHS AND LOWS AS THE VOTES COME IN, WITH THIS REALISTIC, INTERACTIVE 'ELECTION EXPERIENCE' GAME.
WILL YOU BE PRESIDENT?

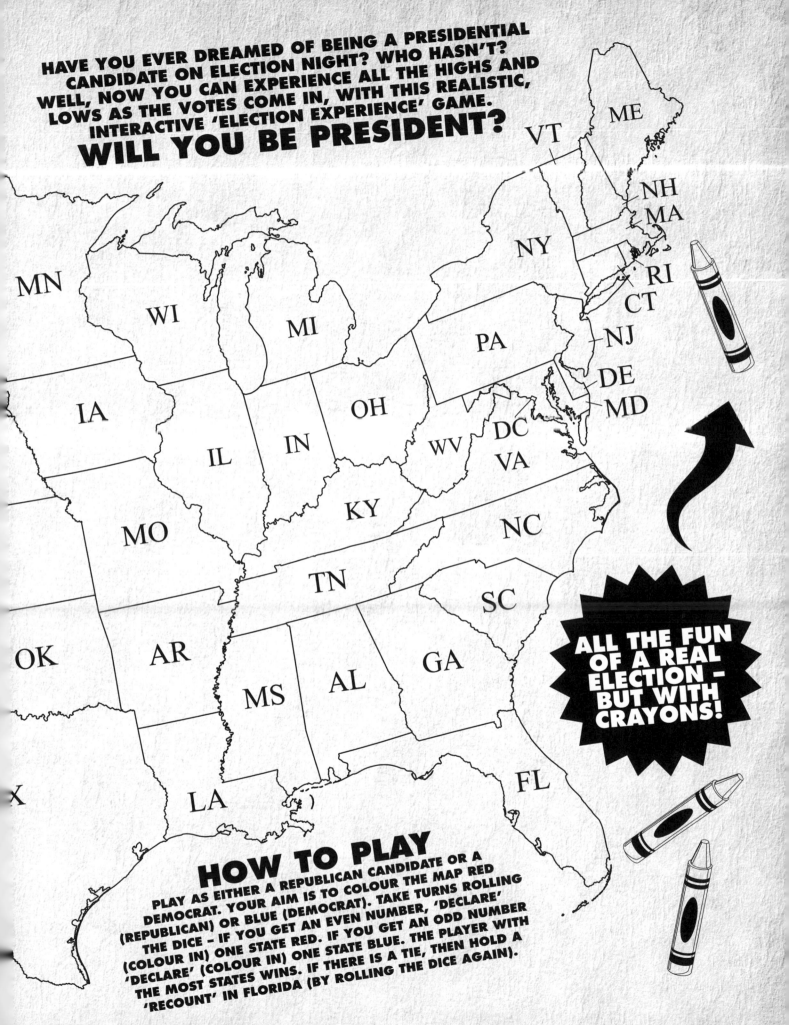

ALL THE FUN OF A REAL ELECTION – BUT WITH CRAYONS!

HOW TO PLAY
PLAY AS EITHER A REPUBLICAN CANDIDATE OR A DEMOCRAT. YOUR AIM IS TO COLOUR THE MAP RED (REPUBLICAN) OR BLUE (DEMOCRAT). TAKE TURNS ROLLING THE DICE – IF YOU GET AN EVEN NUMBER, 'DECLARE' (COLOUR IN) ONE STATE RED. IF YOU GET AN ODD NUMBER 'DECLARE' (COLOUR IN) ONE STATE BLUE. THE PLAYER WITH THE MOST STATES WINS. IF THERE IS A TIE, THEN HOLD A 'RECOUNT' IN FLORIDA (BY ROLLING THE DICE AGAIN).

DELICIOUSLY DONALD
DIPLOMATIC DINNERS

President Trump regularly hosts important diplomatic guests from all around the world. And when it comes to meal times, he likes to treat them to a little fine dining, Trump-style. After extensive research, we've imagined the culinary delights a visiting dignitary might expect to enjoy at the table of the 45th President, so that you can enjoy them for yourself at home.

Amuse-bouche

The delectable marriage of crunchy puffed cornmeal batons enrobed in essence de fromage.

Hors d'Oeuvre

Pan-seared free-range egg served on a toasted, flat, yeast-leavened bread on a bed of premium American cheese and Canadian-style maple-cured ham.

— *or* —

Casserole of freshly-made durum wheat curly tubes, seasoned and baked in a luxurious American cheese and Béchamel-style sauce.

Main course

Rondelle of re-sculpted premium American ground steak, seasoned and seared, and served on a chaise of crisp lettuce, fresh tomato and deluxe American cheese, surrounded by a lightly flame-toasted, sesame-encrusted petit pain.

— or —

Freshly-baked triangular segments of Italian flatbread, adorned with ripened, oregano-seasoned traditional passata sauce and molten cheese garnish (served without crust).

All served with finely cut, delicately sautéed potato spears 'en sac'

Dessert

Traditional American apple pie.   *— or —*   A platter of American cheese.

Beverages

An exotic cocktail of carbonated water and artificial sweeteners, with a secret blend of natural flavourings.

THE GREAT TRUMP CLONE HUNT GAME

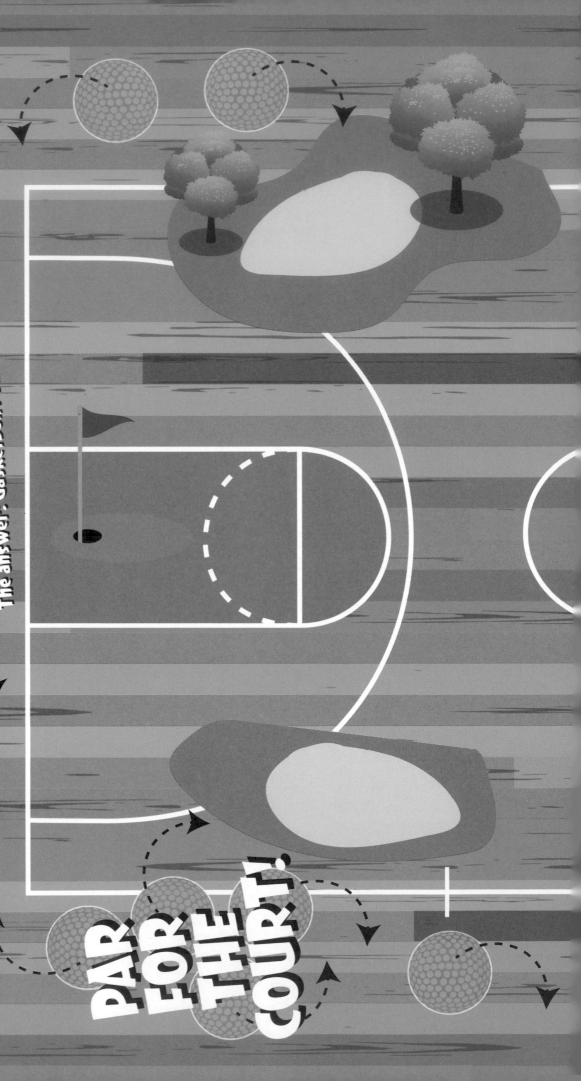

TRUMP'S GASKETBOLF GAME

Donald Trump and Barack Obama have never seen eye to eye.
Donald loves golf, for example, while Barack loves basketball.
So how could we unite these two great presidents?
The answer: Gasketbolf! The clever fusion of 'basketball' and 'golf'.

PAR FOR THE COURT!

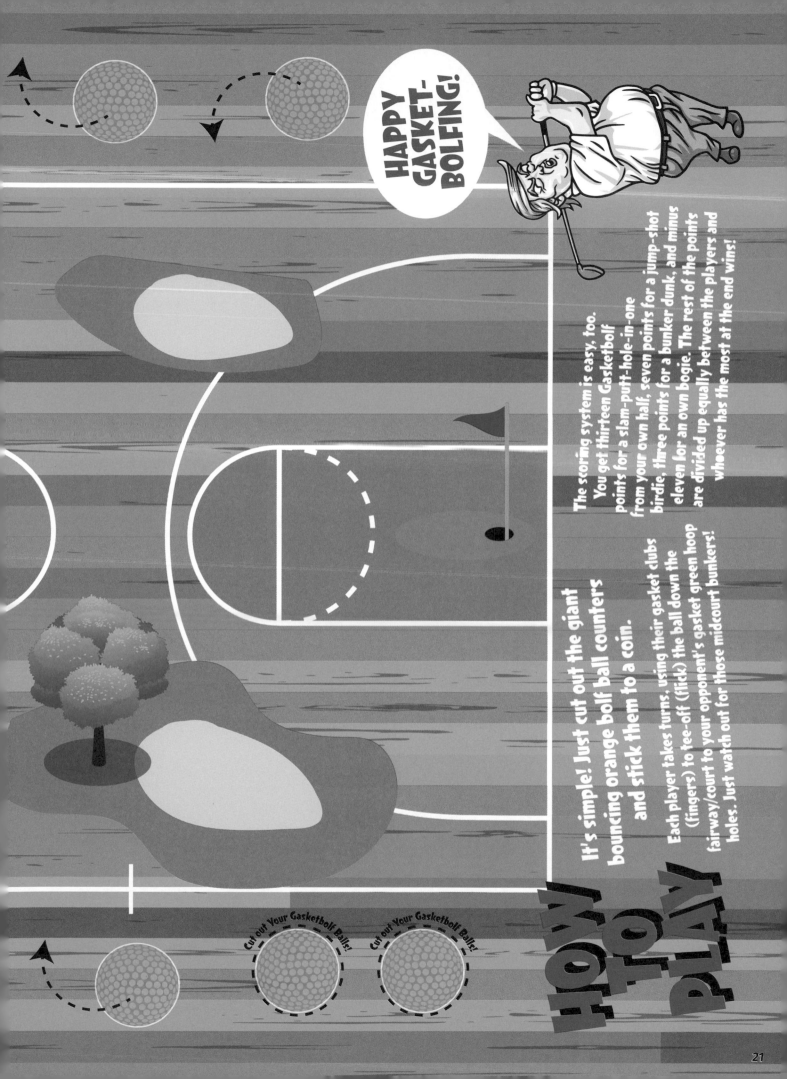

HAPPY GASKET-BOLFING!

HOW TO PLAY

It's simple! Just cut out the giant bouncing orange bolf ball counters and stick them to a coin.

Each player takes turns, using their gasket clubs (fingers) to tee-off (flick) the ball down the fairway/court to your opponent's gasket green hoop or court. Just watch out for those midcourt bunkers and holes!

The scoring system is easy, too. You get thirteen Gasketbolf points for a slam-putt-hole-in-one from your own half, seven points for a jump-shot birdie, three points for a bunker dunk, and minus eleven for an own bogie. The rest of the points are divided up equally between the players and whoever has the most at the end wins!

Cut out Your Gasketbolf Balls!

Cut out Your Gasketbolf Balls!

21

Mr. POTUS Head

Like Donald Trump, all US presidents have their political strengths and weaknesses.

But what if you were able to put together the ultimate president, using only the best bits of previous presidents? Well, now you can with this fun Mr Potus Head ultimate 'Head of State' head game!

Simply cut out the parts you want and place them onto the blank Potus Head below.

Now all you need are some ultimate policies to go with your ultimate president!

TRUMP'S QUIFF

RONALD REAGAN'S COWBOY HAT

BILL CLINTON'S CIGAR

GEORGE W. BUSH'S EYES

WASHINGTON'S WIG

TEDDY'S 'TACHE & GLASSES

NIXON'S NOSE

JFK'S TOOTHY GRIN

ABE LINCOLN'S MOUSTACHELESS BEARD

OBAMA'S EARS

THE MAGICAL JOY OF

Trumpfulness

EVERYBODY'S TALKING ABOUT TRUMPFULNESS, BUT WHAT EXACTLY IS IT?

Trumpfulness is a state of mind, a way of being. It's about allowing yourself to provide your body and mind with everything it desires, regardless of what anybody else thinks or wants. But you don't have to be President of the United States to achieve Trumpfulness.

Just follow our simple steps below and you too can become truly Trumpful.

STEP 1

Own your own Reality

Just because something isn't true, it doesn't mean that you can't make it true. Never let facts get in your way. Remember – your truth is the real truth. If you say it, then it is so.

STEP 2

Build walls, not bridges

Protect yourself from negative outside forces and those who want to disrupt or dilute your personal oasis. Create a sanctuary of peace and safety for yourself, and bathe in a lake of pure you.

STEP 3

Nourish your body and your soul

Feed yourself the richest experience you can have. Remember — the goodness that you put into your body will enrich your spirit, while the impurities will be released through your tunnel of negativity.

STEP 4

Bask in your own glow

Bathe in the sun's goodfulness and reflect its power and golden aura through your own complexion. To feel the sun you must become the sun, and shine as bright as the sun.

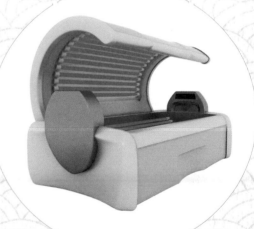

STEP 5

Think Trump, be Trumpful!

Never forget: you matter more than anybody else. So, capitalise on your inner wealth, protect your fortress of youness, gorge upon the banquet of your ego, and exult in your golden aura. Only then can you fully embrace your potential Trumpfulness.

TRUMPCRAFT

PRESIDENTIAL EDITION

AN IMMERSIVE NATION-BUILDING COMPUTER-STYLE SIMULATION GAME

The game in which **YOU** are the pixelated President of the USA. Use your scissors to cut out the axe, then use the axe (or just your scissors again) to 'mine' the items you need to make America great again the way **YOU** want it. You can either play in co-op mode or Republican versus Democrat mode.

A SO, SO BIG WALL

AGRICULTURAL REFORM

AMERICAN INDUSTRY

McBURGERS

ZOMBIES

A DEFENCE BUDGET

A CONSTITUTION

# NOW START BUILDING!

THE 'DONALD OF DESTINY' HOROSCOPES

As the brightest star in the political firmament, Donald has had to keep his gaze fixed firmly on the future of the Western world. But what if he could forecast your future, too? Using huge computers and futuristic terminology, we predict what Donald would predict, if he were to predict your future.

ARIES

March 21 – April 19

Strong-willed, ambitious and passionate

A massive bulbous lunar event in late July, just as Aquarius ascends the space invader. Jupiter rejects an emotional Scorpio from August backwards through August, making you ever more psychic.
Only blue on June 11th.

PROMINENT PRESIDENTIAL ARIANS
Thomas Jefferson

TAURUS

April 20 – May 20

Generous, stubborn and selfish

In the summer month of winter, Mars is retrospect in early Aquarius, and then Apricorns, and then the other ones. Realign and reproduce great magnetic energy up and at 'em.

PROMINENT PRESIDENTIAL TAURUSEANS
Harry S. Truman

GEMINI

May 21 – June 20

Energetic, superficial and impulsive

The Venus principle isn't retrograde from Octoberfest through the first minute to two and a half of November, ending in Libra, impacts your tooth more. Love will resolve unnecessarily.

PROMINENT PRESIDENTIAL GEMINAUGHTS
Donald Trump

CANCER

June 21 – July 22

Loyal, moody, self-pitying

Your Bruno Mars attack is retractable from its upgrade late June through later in later June. Life won't always work, young man. Get a grip. Bruno Mars retro in Aquarius and Copernicus encourages you to make your social life and work more sturdy.

PROMINENT PRESIDENTIAL CANCERIANS
George W. Bush

LEO
July 23 – August 22
Ambitious, domineering, melodramatic

When the sun enters Leo, Venus is already there hiding. Hello, there! In October, Venus goes direct to Libra (do not pass go) in November – not too good for your health!

PROMINENT PRESIDENTIAL LEONS
Barack Obama

VIRGO
August 23 – September 22
Helpful, fussy, inflexible

The sun conjoins your modern metal-loving planet, Bluto, which is reasonable. All earth signs of Capricorn are gone, my dear, leaving only despair and sorrow. The sun always shines on TV.

PROMINENT PRESIDENTIAL VIRGINS
Lyndon B. Johnson

LIBRA
September 23 – October 22
Peaceful, superficial, indecisive

Just after Apollo Creed turns lucid in November, your planet Freddie Mercury conjoins masterful Jupiter for five minutes flat. Your high life needs more inflation at this juncture. Behave yourself, Juicy.

PROMINENT PRESIDENTIAL LIBRARIANS
Dwight D. Eisenhower

SCORPIO
October 23 – November 21
Passionate, obsessive, suspicious

Your planet is making a slow transition back and forth and back and forth through Uranus from time to time and time to time. You will resonate well in Wisconsin.

PROMINENT PRESIDENTIAL SCORPIONS
Theodore Roosevelt

SAGITTARIUS
November 22 – December 21
Selfless, independent, unemotional

Weak solar seeds prevent Bruno Mars from fluctuating and undulating during early Thursday. Remove the lunar entry to facilitate a finer illusion of raucous with Saturn. Try another year next year.

PROMINENT PRESIDENTIAL SAGITTARIANS
Franklin Pierce

CAPRICORN
December 22 – January 19
Patient, dictatorial, distrusting

Your Noodle Node is now in Leo now. Events up in your life spin round and backbite in karmic reverse. A partial solar eclipse in August could affect your bowels. Home sweet home.

PROMINENT PRESIDENTIAL CAPRICOTS
Richard Nixon

AQUARIUS
January 20 – February 18
Witty, unemotional, sarcastic

The all-splicing Bruno Mars-Neptune conglomerate in Gemini may tug at your coat tails, but when Sportacus gets going, the Sun is joined by Crockett and Tubbs. Jupiter and Mercury prizes await!

PROMINENT PRESIDENTIAL AQUARIUMS
Abraham Lincoln

PISCES
February 19 – March 20
Compassionate, indecisive, self-pitying

Saturn is upper retrograde in Capricorn One from April/June/July until early next September/October/November. Late August and early last September will be much too electric times for you.

PROMINENT PRESIDENTIAL PESCETARIANS
George Washington

HOW 'DONALD' ARE YOU?

EVERYBODY WANTS TO BE LIKE DONALD TRUMP THESE DAYS, BUT HAVE YOU EVER WONDERED JUST HOW MUCH LIKE DONALD YOU REALLY ARE?

Well, now you can scientifically discover exactly how 'Donald' you are, simply by answering the questions (*below*) then referring to the answers box (*below the questions below*) to see how high you score on the Trump-o-meter (*next to the answers below the questions below*).

1. It's your birthday and a kindly relative has sent you a crisp $50 bill. Do you:

- ☐ A) Keep $25 but donate the other $25 to someone less fortunate to help pay for their healthcare?
- ☐ B) Get your secret service to quietly dispose of the kindly relative and deny all knowledge of any $50 bill?
- ☐ C) Invest the $50 in real estate and become a billionaire?

2. Your parents have lifted your ban on using social media. Do you:

- ☐ A) Post a surprisingly great Spotify playlist online?
- ☐ B) Get a load of bots to fill everyone's Facebook feeds with fake news to destabilise Western democracy?
- ☐ C) Tweet every random thought that pops into your brain with zero filter?

3. Your parents have gone away for the weekend, leaving you in charge. Do you:

- ☐ A) Enjoy a quiet weekend watching the Chicago White Sox game, and developing shows for Netflix?
- ☐ B) Hold an impromptu judo tournament in your home, to show off your black-belt skills?
- ☐ C) Invite everyone round to your place for a big party, but operate a no-Muslim entry ban?

4. You want to ask your sweetheart to the Prom. Do you:

- ❏ A) Serenade her (*or him*) with an impromptu a capella rendition of Al Green's 'Let Stay Together'?

- ❏ B) Impress her (*or him*) by taking off your shirt and riding a horse as a display of your virility?

- ❏ C) Take a porn star instead and get her to sign a nondisclosure agreement?

5. Your neighbour needs his picket fence whitewashed. Do you:

- ❏ A) Help your neighbour maintain his fence and attempt to negotiate free trade agreements with him?

- ❏ B) Smash down the fence and instigate the annexation of your neighbour's property by declaring it as part of your own Federation?

- ❏ C) Build a great big wall to keep your neighbour off your property instead?

6. Your parents are letting you decorate your bedroom any way you want. Do you:

- ❏ A) Put a basketball hoop above your bed and adorn the walls with pictures of the Chicago Bulls?

- ❏ B) Fill the room with stuffed animals that you've hunted and shot yourself?

- ❏ C) Turn your room into a fully-interactive virtual golf simulator at taxpayer's expense?

ANSWERS

For each question, answering 'A' scores you one point, answering 'B' scores you two points and answering 'C' scores you five points. Work out what you scored for each question, then add up your total score.

If you score **6–8**, then you're an Obama – the opposite of a Trump. Better luck next time!

If you score **9–17**, then you're a Putin – one of Trump's best frenemies. Close, but not quite close enough!

If you score **18-plus** then you're just like the big man himself! And if you score the maximum 30 points, then congratulations: you are Donald Trump!

31

41 GEORGE H. W. "BURNIN'" BUSH

CATCHPHRASE: "Read my lips: it's clobberin' time!"

PHYSICAL STRENGTH:

NEMESIS: Saddam "Evil Mario" Hussein

SIGNATURE MOVE: Bushwhacker Back Fist

APOCALYPSE RATING:

WORLD WRESTLING PRESIDENTS

42

SMOKIN' BILL CLINTON

CATCHPHRASE: "I ain't no sucker - you're the sucker"

PHYSICAL STRENGTH:

NEMESIS: Himself

SIGNATURE MOVE: The Big Bill Low-Blow

APOCALYPSE RATING:

WORLD WRESTLING PRESIDENTS

TRUMP TREK

SPACE. THE FINAL FRONTIER. THESE ARE THE VOYAGES
OF THE STARSHIP TRUMPERPRISE. ITS FOUR-YEAR MISSION:
TO BUILD NEW WALLS AND KEEP OUT NEW CIVILIZATIONS.
TO BOLDLY GO WHERE NO TRUMP HAS GONE BEFORE!

BY ARTHUR C. SAW

Captain Donald J. Trump was the heroic and highly intelligent leader of Space Force, a special new futuristic arm of the US military, entirely invented by Captain Trump himself to help make space great again, and to prevent space murderers, drug dealers and illegal aliens from invading Planet Earth and stealing human jobs.

On the border between outer space and the Earth, everything seemed peaceful enough. But on the bridge of the Starship *Trumperprise*, Captain Trump examined the inky blackness with a sceptical eye.

'Captain's log, Space Date eleven, three, twenty twenty,' said the heroic space billionaire to no one in particular. 'Something's very, very, very wrong out there. It's so, so quiet today. *Too quiet, actually.*' Suddenly he spun around to his crew. 'Mr Pence, set scanners to search on all known frequencies.'

'Affirmative, Captain,' said Pence, Captain Trump's highly logical, strangely unemotional, white-haired second in command.

'Captain, we're picking up a reading on space frequency alpha,' said Lieutenant Huckabee Sanders, Captain Trump's Chief Communications Officer. 'It's very faint but it appears to be coming from the dark side of the Moon.'

'The Pink Floyd album?' asked Pence, logically.

'No, Mr Pence,' said Captain Trump, gravely. 'She means the actual dark side of the actual Moon. It must be Chinese Moon Robots. Let's beam down to the surface to investigate.'

Captain Trump bravely volunteered himself to lead the away party. With him went his trusty, logical number two, Pence, along with three faceless crew members, who wore futuristic red space shirts to show that they were expendable.

The team stepped into the transporter device that conveniently teleported people down to the surface of various planets and saved money on the special-effects budget. Chief Engineer Pompeo operated the transporter's controls and soon the Space Force personnel rematerialised on the surface of the Moon. Sadly, however, something went wrong with the transporter beam and one of the red-shirted crew members was instantly vaporised upon arrival.

'Ooops! Sorry about that,' said Chief Engineer Pompeo over the intercom.

'Captain Trump,' said one of the other expendable red-shirted crew members. 'I think I've found something.'

Sure enough, the unimportant crew member held up a piece of unmistakably non-American steel.

'Just as I thought – Chinese Moon Robots,' said the handsome, wise space captain as he ran a hand through his thick, manly blond hair, thoughtfully. 'But wait. These robot scraps are very, very, very old. *Too old, actually...*'

to have made those transmissions we picked up on our scanners.'

'In that case, Captain,' said Pence unemotionally, 'it is logical to assume that somebody else was responsible.'

'Precisely, Mr Pence,' said Captain Trump. 'Once again, your invaluable analytical brain has cleverly worked out the correct answer.'

But before he could heap any more unnecessary praise on his loyal deputy, their discussion was interrupted by the loud sound of a laser-gun blast, as another of the expendable crew members was predictably disintegrated before their very eyes.

'Someone appears to be shooting at us, Captain,' said Pence, perceptively.

'Quick! Behind that moon rock!' ordered Captain Trump. They all leapt for cover.

Captain Trump bravely surveyed the scene with a set of futuristic space binoculars. And, as the smooth alien quiff of a portly extra-terrestrial figure in a nearby moon crater slowly came into focus, Captain Trump's worst fears were confirmed. It was his arch-frenemy – the Supreme Leader of the ruthless, warlike alien race, the Kimjongs. Captain Trump stepped out from behind the moon rock, holding his tiny hands in the air to show he meant no harm.

'yavDaq qamDu'Daj lIS Say' jIH!' he said in the mother tongue of the Kimjong Empire.

'What do you mean, your trousers are in the wash?' asked the villainous alien warlord, bemused.

'I'm sorry, my Kimjong is a little rusty,' explained the healthily tanned businessman-slash-space buccaneer. 'I was trying to suggest that we hold a summit somewhere – like maybe Singapore – to shake hands a lot in front of cameras and discuss sanctions without really coming to any conclusions.'

'Never!' cried the rotund, slick-haired alien.

'Okay, well, how about Vietnam, then?' shrugged the captain, generously. 'It's supposed to be very, very, very nice. Plus, I've never been there before, actually, because of my bone spurs.'

But it was no use. The Kimjong warrior fired off another volley of laser-gun blasts at the Space Force team, inevitably vaporising the remaining red-shirted crew member.

'All the expendable ones have now been disintegrated, Captain,' said Pence, astutely. 'I suggest we retreat to the safety of the ship without delay.'

'Beam us up, Pompy!' said the courageous captain into his futuristic space communicator.

The pair dissolved into atomic particles just in time, as the Kimjong Supreme Leader's laser-gun bolt hit a moon rock just were they had been standing.

Back on the bridge of the Starship *Trumperprise*, there was a flurry of activity as Captain Trump heroically returned to the space captain's chair.

'Red alert! Shields up, Mr Pence,' ordered Captain Trump. 'Lieutenant Huckabee Sanders, contact Space Force HQ – tell them we're under attack from some very, very, very dangerous Kimjongs.'

'I can't get through to HQ, Captain,' replied Lieutenant Huckabee Sanders. 'We're experiencing heavy Russian interference, sir.'

Just then, the Starship *Trumperprise* was rocked by a massive laser blast.

'That blast came from the Moon,' said Pence, demonstrating his keen observational skills once again.

'Except that's not a Moon,' said Captain Trump, narrowing his wise but naturally young-looking eyes, 'it's some kind of Death Star...'

'We're being hailed by the Kimjong leader,' said Lieutenant Huckabee Sanders as the tyrannical alien's face filled the large space display in front of them.

'That's right, Captain Trump!' he gloated. 'While you were busy patrolling the border for space immigrants, I was cleverly burrowing my way into the Moon's core and converting it into a nuclear Death Star!'

'Evasive manoeuvre two-three-alpha-covfefe!' barked Captain Trump. The starship's crew wrestled with the controls, but it was too late. Another space-laser blast, even more powerful than the last, shook the ship, sending a series of explosions rippling across the hull.

'Status report!' shouted Captain Trump through the smoke and sparks that now filled the bridge.

'Shields are down, Captain,' said Chief Engineer Pompeo. 'We have hull breaches in sections four, eight and ten. Space engines and weapons systems are offline.'

'Damn it!' exclaimed the captain. 'We're sitting ducks! Mr Pence, is there anything we can—' But as the blond-haired space lothario turned to his trusty number two, he saw that his vice-captain's chair was empty.

'Captain Trump!' came the voice of a nameless but almost certainly red-shirted crew member over the ship's space intercom system. 'It's Mr Pence, sir. He's down here in engineering. He has entered the space engine room without any protective equipment!' continued the anonymous actor, as he inexplicably exploded.

'No!' shouted Trump, leaping from his captain's chair with extreme agility, demonstrating his incredible physical fitness, despite a largely unhealthy diet and lack of significant exercise.

'Captain, we're reading an energy surge from the surface of the Moon. The Kimjongs are powering their Death Star!' exclaimed Lieutenant Huckabee Sanders.

'We cannae take another attack, Cap'n!' said Chief Engineer Pompeo in a suddenly incomprehensible Scottish accent.

But Captain Trump was already halfway to engineering. Just as he got there, he saw his faithful friend behind the plexiglass safety screen that separated the space engine's nuclear core from the rest of the bay.

'Pence!' he shouted. 'What the hell are you doing?'

'My job, Captain,' said the white-haired stalwart, already suffering from the effects of space radiation. 'As vice-captain of this Space Force vessel, it is my job to make space great again, so I am going to manually eject our nuclear space-engine core and use it as a bomb to destroy that Kimjong Death Star.'

'But you'll die!' said Captain Trump, helplessly.

'It is the only logical course of action, Captain,' said Pence, rationally.

'Five seconds until the Kimjong Death Star weapon is fully powered, Captain,' Chief Engineer Pompeo's now fully Scottish voice came over the intercom.

Captain Trump's eyes filled with tears as he reached out with one tiny hand to touch the plexiglass screen that separated him from his dependable second-in-command. 'Mr Pence – we have been, and always will be, brothers in arms.'

'The Dire Straits album?' asked Pence, confused.

'No, Mr Pence. Actual brothers in actual arms.'

'Live long and prosper at the expense of others,' said Mister Pence, weakly.

'Mr Pence,' said Captain Trump, fighting back the tears. 'You're fired.'

Mr Pence smiled at Captain Trump's joke, displaying a human emotion for the first time ever. Then he pressed the space button that opened the space doors and ejected the space engine into space. Both Pence and the nuclear core were sucked out into the cold vacuum and went tumbling towards the surface of the Moon-slash-Death Star.

'Goodbye, my old friend,' said Captain Trump, pouting with statesmanlike dignity.

Meanwhile, on the dark side of the Moon (the actual Moon, not the album), the Kimjong Supreme Leader stood with his chubby finger poised over the big red button that controlled the powerful Death Star weapon, ready to deal the final blow to his arch-frenemy. But before his hand could reach the button, there was a massive explosion as the nuclear core from the *Trumperprise* collided with the Death Star, setting off a chain reaction that caused the entire Moon to explode into space dust.

On the bridge of the Starship *Trumperprise*, Captain Donald J. Trump surveyed the battlefield.

'Great work, guys,' said the captain, proudly. 'We wiped out the Kimjongs and we nuked the Moon. Once again, Space Force has been very, very, very successful. *Completely* successful, actually.'

'Go, Space Force!' cheered the crew in celebration.

'Go, Space Force!' echoed Captain Trump heroically, as he gave the Space Force flag a big, strange hug.

THE END

my huggable president

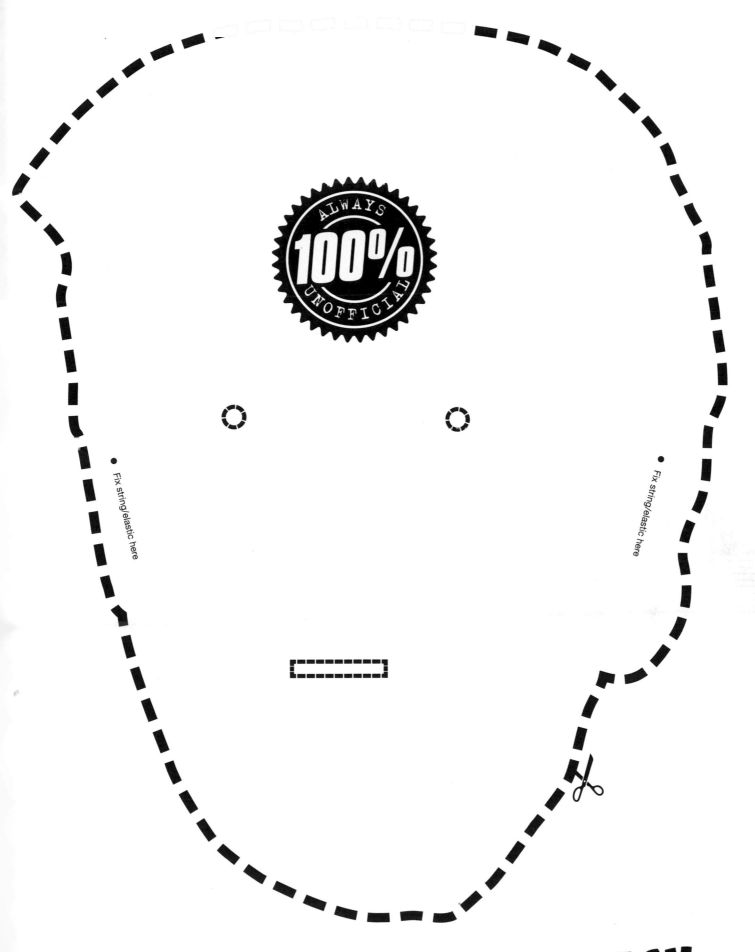

ALWAYS 100% UNOFFICIAL

Fix string/elastic here

Fix string/elastic here

Donald Trump!

FUN MASK

Donald Trump!

FUN MASK

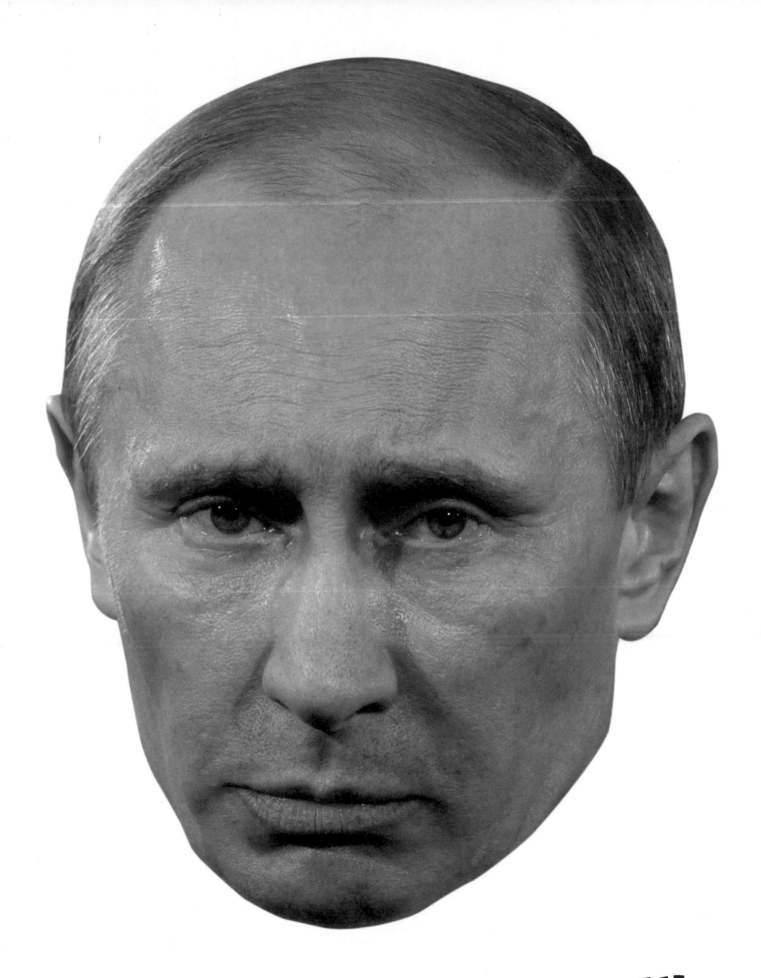

Vladimir Putin!

FUN MASK

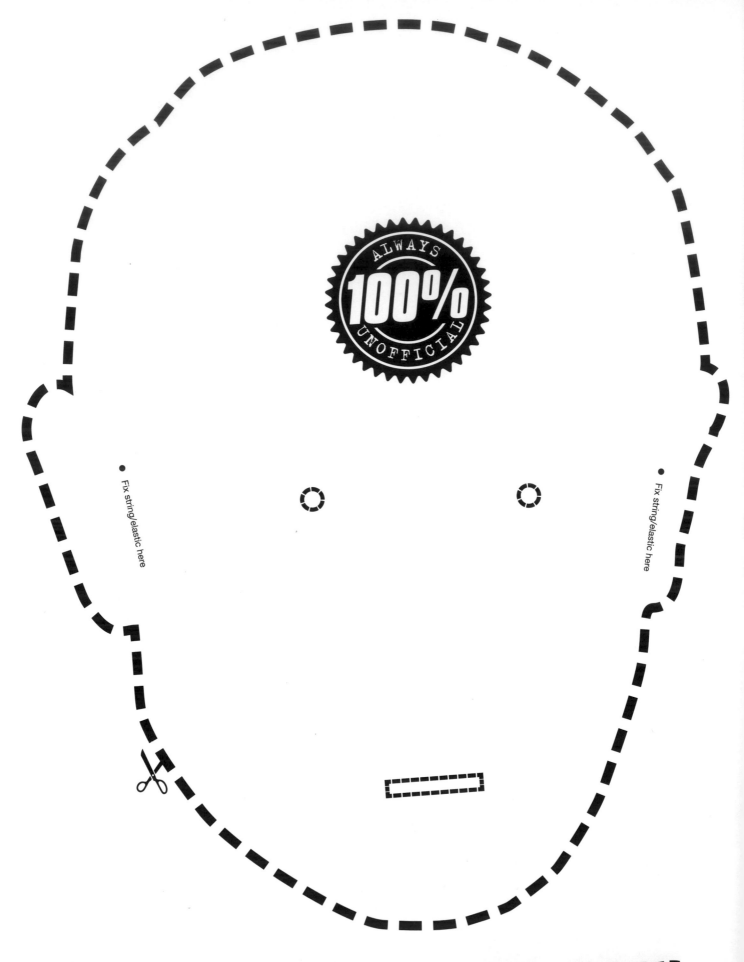

Fix string/elastic here

Fix string/elastic here

Vladimir Putin! FUN MASK

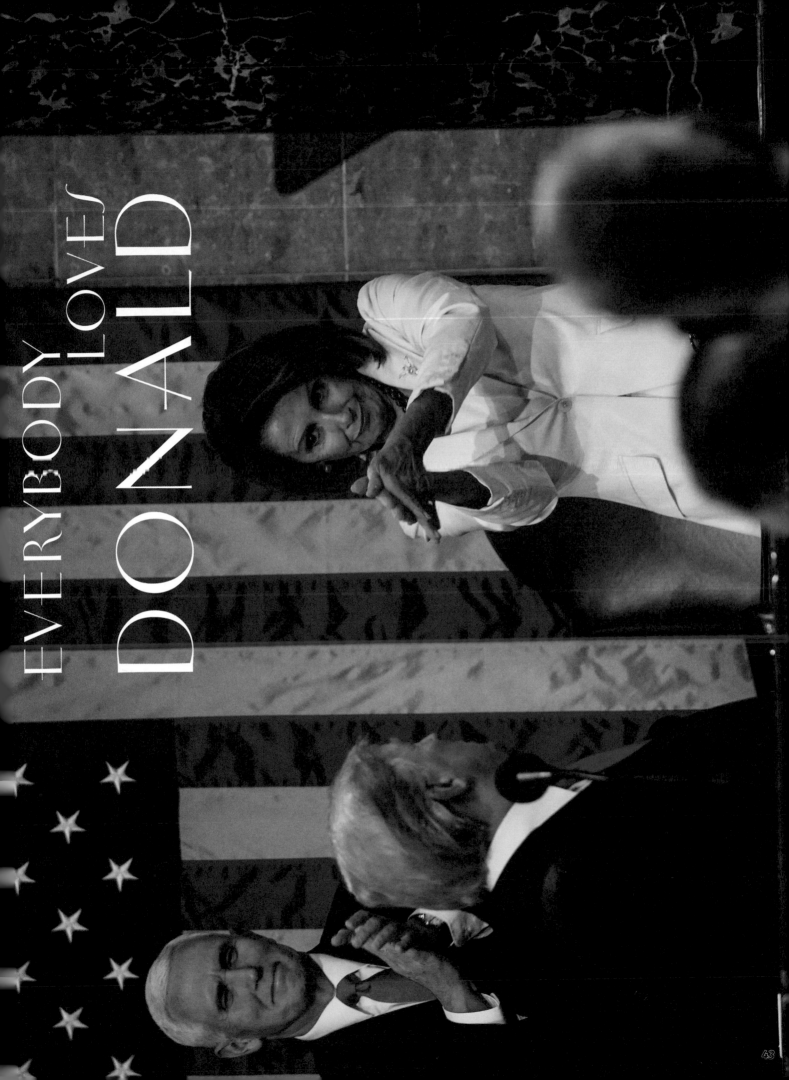

EVERYBODY LOVES
DONALD

43

GLUE

CUT OUT

TRUMP-BOT

DONALD J.

BATTLING
ROBOTS

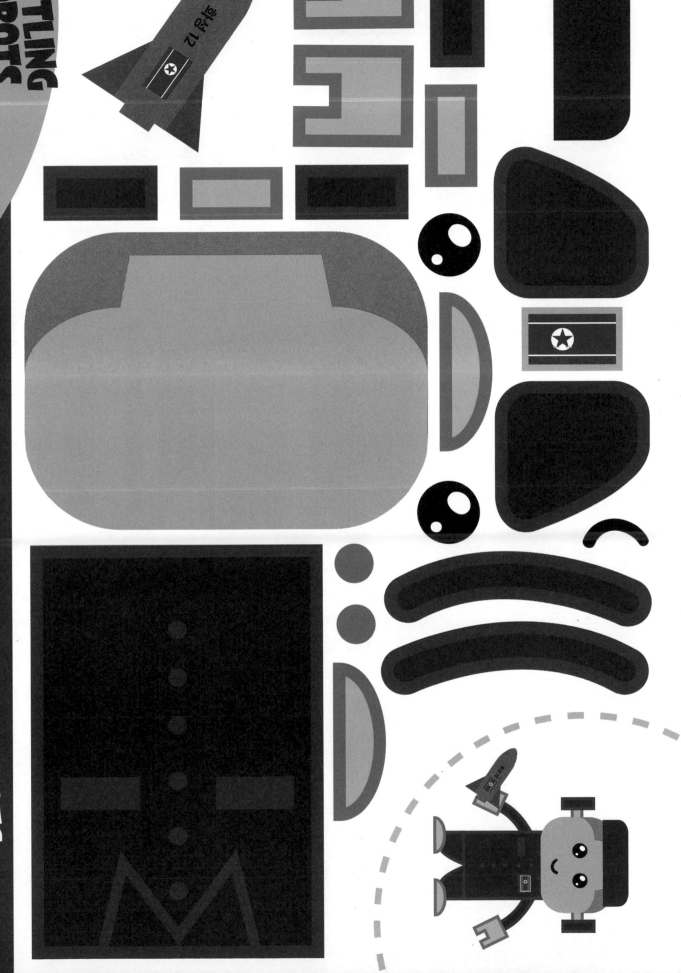

KIM-BOT JONG-UN

COMPLETE YOUR ROBOTS
AND LET BATTLE COMMENCE!

45

DONALD'S PARTY GAMES

Donald's a member of the Republican Party but he also likes to throw amazing birthday parties. Imagine you've been invited to one of Donald's get-togethers. Here's a selection of some of the party games you might well find yourself playing.

1

TAX YOUR NEIGHBOUR

Each party guest is given a post-it note with a tax rate on it, which they must stick on their own forehead without looking at it. Players have to deduce how much they owe the US government by taking turns to ask questions. Those who guess correctly win tax breaks for the following fiscal twelve-month.

PIN THE BLAME ON THE DEMOCRAT

Place a picture of a Democratic donkey onto a wall. Each player must wear a blindfold and randomly pin their own political failures onto the donkey's butt. Whoever makes the blame stick wins.

2

3

TUG OF ACTUAL WAR

Divide the party guests into two teams and separate the area into two territories – one is America, the other is North Korea. Both teams must pull on either end of a rope, until America wins.

4

PASS THE BILL THROUGH THE CONGRESS

Everyone sits in a big circle and passes a bill of rights around while music plays. When the music stops, whoever is holding the bill tries to get it through Congress. When the music starts, the whole process begins again. The game ends when either the bill is finally passed, or Donald declares a national emergency.

5

WHACK-A-GOVERNMENT-MOLE

One player is a secret mole, feeding information back to the Russian President and creating fake news, in order to destabilise Western democracy. Interrogate each other using UN-sanctioned enhanced interrogation techniques and, once the mole has been identified, hire a covert government agency to whack him.

TWITTER TWISTER

Exactly like a traditional game of Twister, where you spin the dial and place your feet and hands where instructed – except that players must keep one hand on a cell phone at all times, in order to tweet out inane boasts, random statistics and unrelated gibberish over social media.

6

YOU BE

YOUR FACE HERE

THE
DONALD

WHAT WOULD IT FEEL LIKE TO BE A PRESIDENT?
WHAT WOULD IT FEEL LIKE TO BE A TRUMP?
CAN YOU IMAGINE?

WELL, IMAGINE NO MORE. SIMPLY PASTE A PHOTO OF YOUR FACE ONTO THE SPACE WHERE DONALD'S FACE SHOULD BE IN THE FACE-SPACE OPPOSITE AND YOU CAN BECOME AN INSTANT PRESIDENT TRUMP!

PRESIDENTIAL DECREE

My President name is President _ _ _ _ _ _ _ _ _ _ _ _ _
Trump and here is my presidential decree.

"I hereby ban_ _ _ _ _ _ _ _ _ _ _ _ _ _ from my country"

"Everyone must pay $_ _ _ _ _ _ for healthcare"

"I will build a big, big _ _ _ _ _ _ _ _ _ _ _ _ _ _ _ _ _ _"

"I henceforth decree free burgers for all _ _ _ _ _ _ _ _ _
and NFL players"

"I will reduce corporate taxes by _ _ _ _ _ _ _%"

"Compulsory golf for all _ _ _ _ _ _ _ _ _ _ _ _ _ _ _ _"

"I will make _ _ _ _ _ _ _ _ _ _ _ compulsory for all immigrants"

"I will make _ _ _ _ _ _ _ _ _ _ _ _ _ _ great again"

OTHER
PRESIDENTS

PUTIN

This action-packed President of the Russian Federation (Russia) is not only Russia's most important man, he's also a keen sportsman and martial artist. So, if he ever played President Trump at golf, Vladimir would almost certainly get his "putt in" (Putin). And if he ever played him at martial arts, then "judo" (you'd know) what the result would be!

MACRON

This president is the President of France, so he has a French name: Emmanuel Macron. Although this 41-year-old president is French, when he visits the States, he (probably) likes to have a Big Mac(ron) and (French) fries!

CHEESE

France has another president – but this one's made of French cheese. Because it's the French cheese 'President'. This 50-year-old President doesn't rule any countries, but it does rule the taste buds with its cheesy flavour (when you eat it).

THOMAS J. WHITMORE

This American President isn't even a president – he's an American actor called Bill Pullman, who played an American President who fought for American independence against illegal aliens from space in the cleverly prophetic film *Independence Day*.

This President has four wheels (five if you count the spare (six if you count the steering wheel)), because it's a car. This 92-year-old retired President from Indiana will 'drive' you crazy with excitement (if you can get it to go fast enough).

STUDEBAKER

THE PRESIDENT

If you think that Canada doesn't have a president, you'd be wrong. It has a Prime Minister (Justin Trudeau) and a president – or rather The President, the 10,296-foot peak of a mountain range in the Canadian Rockies. Except this Canadian giant doesn't have a 'rocky' relationship with (President) Donald Trump!

Donald's All-You-Can-Eat Word Salad

Help yourself to ingredients from Donald's all-you-can-eat word salad bar, give them a toss and arrange them onto the empty plate to create your own delicious, healthy Trump salad sentences.

For example, tomato, tomato, rocket, cucumber = so, so big wall.

TRUMP TATTOO SOURCEBOOK

DONALD WANTS TO BUILD A WALL TO LEAVE A PERMANENT REMINDER OF HIS PRESIDENCY, BUT HOW CAN YOU PERMANENTLY REMIND YOURSELF OF TRUMP'S PRESIDENTIAL LEGACY?

WHY NOT CHOOSE ONE OF THESE STYLISH DESIGNS TO USE FOR INSPIRATION AND HEAD DOWN TO YOUR LOCAL TATTOO PARLOUR?

PRESIDENT TRUMP
HISTORY BOOK
LADDER GAME

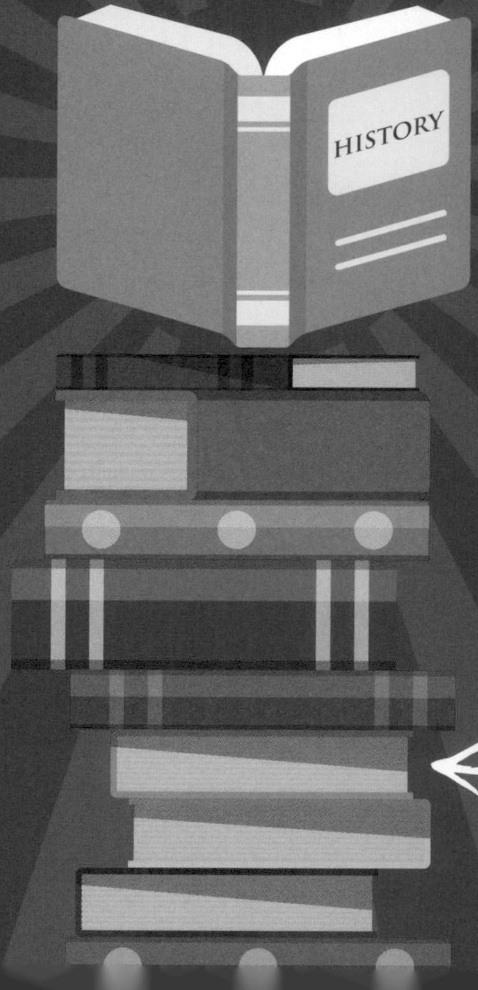

GREAT EXPECTATIONS
Your approval rating has gone up by two points
GO UP
TWO BOOKS

HISTORY

BIOGRAPHY

Imagine you and your opponent are presidents of the USA.

Like Donald Trump, you are racing to get your legacy into the history books. Cut out the hungry, hungry bookworms below, and roll the dice to eat your way up the book ladder and see who gets there first! Land on a bonus book and you could end up taking the lead ...

But watch out for those presidential pitfalls!

GONE WITH THE WIND
It turns out climate change is a thing after all
GO DOWN TWO BOOKS

DOCTOR ZHIVAGO
Your predecessor's affordable healthcare act has been repealed in Congress
GO UP TWO BOOKS

WAR AND PEACE
You start a war with North Korea
GO DOWN THREE BOOKS

FIFTY SHADES OF GREY
You've been embroiled in a sex scandal with a Playboy model
GO DOWN TWO BOOKS

America's Next Top President!

Hey! You've got Trump-a-mail! Donald Trump has proved that almost anyone can be President of the United States. But it's not as easy as it looks. You need political support, a bitchin' election campaign and to be next-level fierce. Here's our selection of the most flawsome candidates around.

But remember – only one of them will become America's Next Top President.

Mike Pence

He might play second fiddle to the Big D, but Mike's the one who wows us on the catwalk. He mustn't rest on his dazzling smile, though.

He's gotta work that vice presidential booty if he wants to be numero uno!

Bernie Sanders

With his effortless, shabby chic style, Bernie's got it down. This guy proves that age ain't nothing but a number (in his case, 77).

OMG, Bernie – you got sass on yo ass!

Joe Biden

Joe is the classic all-American boy next door with a bubble-gum smile – put him on the cover of *Vogue* and this guy's gonna break some hearts.

Time for this sexy sidekick to step up!

Elizabeth Warren

This Democratic diva has got that whole 'she got it going on' thing going on. She could be queen of the fashion houses and

queen of the White House!

Kylo Ren

Boy, does this kid have some serious attitude. He's already a prime candidate for Supreme Leader of the First Order but with a light side makeover, he could be a prime candidate for America's Next Top President.

Go, Kylo, go!

Vladimir Putin

Tanned and toned, Vlad's just as fierce at a political summit as he is on a swimwear shoot. Some say he's already running the country – either way,

Vlad's da bomb!

1950s
The Ol' Blue Eyes

1970s
The Diana Ross

1960s
The Presley

1980s
The Flock
of Seagulls

1990s
The Fresh Prince

2000s
The Green Day

2010s
The Beyonce

Donald's TOP OF THE FOPS
HAIR FLAIR
HISTORY CHAIR

Donald knows a thing or two about hair. His iconic quiff is the envy of men — and women! — all over the world. But Donald also knows that to be a successful President of the United States, he must learn from great popular hairstyles of the past. And who better to learn from than pop's top fops?

That's why Donald has taken a seat in the barber's chair of pop musical history to travel on a journey of hirsute discovery.

TEN-MINUTE TEATIME

Trump-Teaser

DONALD DOESN'T DRINK TEA, preferring instead a cool Diet Coke. But if he did, he'd almost certainly enjoy a cuppa whilst completing a quick afternoon brain work-out. You too can be like a brew-sipping, word-crossing version of Donald, with this tantalising tea-time quickie.

Across

1. _____ Daniels, Trump's alleged lover (6)
4. Trump's daughter (6)
6. Trump's Vice President (5)
8. Trump's political party (10)
9. Beauty pageant once part-owned by Trump – Miss ___
10. Trump's tall building (5)
13. Trump's middle name (4)
14. _____ time (9)

Down

2. Current wife of Trump (7)
3. Trump's Palm Beach private club (3-1-4)
5. The _____ , Donald's fun hiring show (10)
7. Hillary _____ , Trump's opposition in 2016 (7)
11. Trump's favourite sport (4)
12. Borough of New York where Trump was raised (6)

Donald's 'Executive Time' Tips

Donald knows that when you are a busy president, you need some space in your hectic daily schedule that's devoted just to you. But you don't have to be a busy President of the United States to allocate up to 60% of your working day to unstructured recreational activities. Here are some of the ways that you too can maximise your executive time, just like Donald does!

Play some executive golf

Take some time to tee off in your own, personal, state-of-the-art golf simulator room. Alternatively, why not visit one of the many golf courses you own around the world?

Enjoy an executive lunch

Nutrition is important to keep your strength up for your working day. So, don't be afraid to take some time to chow down at your favourite restaurant. Eating food quickly can be quite exhausting, though, so why not use the rest of your executive lunch time to sleep off your exertions?

Shop online, executively

We all need to treat ourselves from time to time and what better way to relieve the stresses of your busy day than by doing some high street shopping online. Don't know which high street to buy? No problem – just buy 'em all!

Go for an executive drive in the country

De-stress by having your personal driver take you for a long relaxing drive in your executive limousine and enjoy a light nap as your motorcade whistles down the country roads. Alternatively, why not take a ride to a completely different country in your personal jet and have a sleep there instead.

Watch executive TV

Relax and keep yourself up to date with current affairs at the same time by spending large portions of your day in bed, watching Fox News on three TV screens at once. Better still, why not unwind by starring in your very own reality TV show?

43 GEORGE W. "BUSH BABY" BUSH

CATCHPHRASE: "Nobody pets *my* goat!"

PHYSICAL STRENGTH:

NEMESIS: AL "INCONVENIENT AL" GORE

SIGNATURE MOVE: The Texan Toejam

APOCALYPSE RATING:

WORLD WRESTLING PRESIDENTS

44 — BARACK "HAWAII FIVE" OBAMA

CATCHPHRASE: "Let *me* take Obamacare of this!"

PHYSICAL STRENGTH:

NEMESIS: DONALD "THE DONINATOR" TRUMP

SIGNATURE MOVE: The Barack Attack

APOCALYPSE RATING:

WORLD WRESTLING PRESIDENTS

LET THEM EAT BURGERS!

68

INSERT MEME HERE

Just for fun we imagined what might be Trump's top tunes if he liked music...

NOW THAT'S WHAT I CALL DONALD

Bigly Love
FLEETWOOD MAC

Another Brick in the Wall
PINK FLOYD

Riders on the Stormy
THE DOORS

We Shall Overcomb
MAHALIA JACKSON

White House Rock
ELVIS PRESLEY

(Im)Peaches
THE STRANGLERS

Loco in Mar-a-Lago
THE FOUR TOPS

Son of a Real Estate Developer
DUSTY SPRINGFIELD

China in Your Tiny Hand
T'PAU

Nasty Woman
ROY ORBISON

Black Covfefe in Bed
SQUEEZE

The (Immigrant) Tide Is High
BLONDIE

The Cronicles of Mel-narnia

The Trump the Nasty Woman and the Wardrobe

by
Joy de Vision

nce upon a time, four posh English children from the 1940s were staying with their posh uncle in a big, posh house somewhere in England. The older brother and sister, Peter and Susan, were the sensible grown-up ones; the youngest sister, Lucy, was the quirky one; and Edmund was the spiteful (but ultimately well-meaning) one.

One day, they were all playing a game that posh English children from the 1940s played, which involved climbing inside pieces of furniture. Peter and Susan sensibly climbed into a cupboard. Edmund spitefully climbed into a coal scuttle and Lucy climbed into a big, quirky old wardrobe. But, while the cupboard and the coal scuttle were normal pieces of furniture, the wardrobe wasn't. It was a magic wardrobe with a magic back door in the back that opened up to the magical world of Mel-narnia.

Lucy climbed as deep inside the wardrobe as she could and was confused to find that it was snowing.

'That's strange,' she said to herself. 'It doesn't normally snow inside a wardrobe.'

But that's because she was no longer inside the wardrobe any more. She was now inside the snowy and magical world of Mel-narnia.

There, by a lamppost, Lucy met a group of talking animals, including some beavers and a strange creature who was half goat and half James McAvoy. They told her that the magical world of Mel-narnia was frozen in a perpetual winter because of a Nasty Woman called Hillary Clinton, who had sent some emails. The only person who could save them was Don-aslan, the mighty magical celebrity business-lion with his lustrous mane of blond hair, who was the rightful ruler of all Mel-narnia.

Lucy couldn't believe her ears or her eyes! She returned to the wardrobe and went back to the real world to tell her brothers and sister all about her adventures in Mel-narnia (through the wardrobe). But they all just thought she was telling great big fibs.

'Oh, Lucy,' said sensible Peter. 'You're so quirky! You're always making silly stuff up!'

'Yes, Lucy,' said sensible Susan. 'You've got such an overactive imagination. Animals can't talk! Not even talking beavers!'

'I hate you all and wish you were dead,' said spiteful Edmund.

But Lucy insisted that they all climb inside the wardrobe with her so that they could see for themselves. Peter rolled his eyes.

'Okay then, silly girl,' he said in a patronising voice, winking at Susan. 'Let's all visit this so-called "magical" world of yours, shall we?'

And so, the four children climbed inside the wardrobe.

'It's a bit chilly in here,' complained Peter.

'Is it me, or is it snowing in here a bit?' asked Susan.

'You all smell,' said Edmund.

Luckily there were some warm coats inside the wardrobe, so they put these on to keep them warm from the cold wardrobe snow.

'Look – there's the lamppost!' exclaimed Lucy. 'And there's James McAvoy with some talking beavers!'

'Hello!' said James McAvoy and the beavers.

Now it was Peter, Susan and Edmund's turn to not believe their eyes or their ears!

'See!' said Lucy. 'I wasn't fibbing! There really is a magical world of Mel-narnia inside our uncle's wardrobe.'

'Except,' said a beaver, mournfully, 'if we don't help Don-aslan defeat the Nasty Woman, then the magical world of Mel-narnia could be lost forever.'

'In that case,' said Peter, bravely, 'it's up to us to help Don-aslan make Mel-narnia great again!'

The children went to the beavers' house to make plans. But, while they weren't looking, Edmund slipped away.

'I don't want to help anyone make Mel-narnia great again!' he said to himself. 'I want to eat Turkish Delight instead.'

As he trudged through the snow, Edmund heard a sleigh approaching.

'Hey! Over here!' he called.

The sleigh pulled up beside Edmund and a very democratic-looking woman leaned over to greet him.

'I am Hillary Clinton,' said the woman with a sneer. 'Who are you?'

'I am Edmund from the other side of the wardrobe,' said Edmund. 'Do you have any Turkish Delight?'

'No,' replied Hillary Clinton. 'Why would you even ask that?'

But even though the Nasty Woman didn't have any Turkish Delight, Edmund ignored all the advice he had ever been given about stranger danger and went with her in her sleigh, just to be difficult. And off they sleighed, back to Hillary Clinton's big white house.

Meanwhile, Lucy, Peter and Susan were making a plan with the talking beavers.

'So, what we're going to do,' mansplained Peter, 'is travel across Mel-narnia to meet with the mighty magical celebrity business-lion, Don-aslan, and help him defeat the Nasty Woman.'

'That sounds like a very sensible plan,' said Susan.

'Hold on… has anyone seen Edmund?' asked Lucy quirkily.

'I think I saw him go off in a sleigh with a Nasty Woman,' said a talking beaver.

'Oh my! Then we will need to rescue him, too!' exclaimed Lucy.

'Don't worry,' said James McAvoy, 'Don-aslan will know what to do. He's always tweeting about how he is really, really, really smart and a very stable genius.'

So off they all went on a long and exciting journey to a secret magical golf course, where Don-aslan was gathering all the magical folk of Mel-narnia. All of Don-aslan's friends were eager to meet the children from beyond the wardrobe. Among the colourful characters who greeted them were Jared Kushner, the cheeky talking weasel, and Mike Pence, the talking ass.

Suddenly, a solemn hush fell over the amassed animals as Mike Pompeo, the talking hog, stepped up to a stone table that was in the middle of the golf course for some reason.

'Good folk of Mel-narnia, gracious visitors from the real world – please bow your heads for your rightful ruler, the mighty magical celebrity business-lion, Don-aslan!'

There was a collective gasp of awe from the crowd, as Mike Pompeo, the talking hog, stepped aside. Into the light stepped the most powerful and mentally fit lion the children had ever seen. His lustrous blond mane rippled in the breeze and he looked unimpeachably statesmanlike in the handsome red 'Make Mel-narnia Great Again' baseball cap that he was wearing.

'It's great to see so, so many supporters here today,' said the lion, as he gestured around the amassed crowd with his surprisingly small front paws. 'Remember, folks – when I'm in charge, I promise big, big cuts to corporate tax rates and I'll also build a yuge wall to keep the talking Chihuahuas and other Mexican animals out!'

'Whoo, hoo!' whooped Michael Cohen, the talking pitbull, and Brett Kavanaugh, the talking snake.

Don-aslan approached the children. Peter, who had decided he was in charge, stepped up and kneeled before the great, wise, mentally competent ruler.

'Oh, mighty Don-aslan,' said Peter, as his sisters joined him in kneeling before their host, 'we humble non-magical humans pledge ourselves to your cause. Together, we will help you defeat the Nasty Woman and restore greatness to your magical land.'

But, no sooner had the children vowed their support, than a loud, evil, democratic cackling laughter interrupted the solemn moment. The group turned to find Hillary Clinton, the Nasty Woman, had arrived on her sleigh, with spiteful Edmund at her side.

'You fools!' scoffed Hillary. 'Don-aslan will never be the ruler of Mel-narnia!' And with that, she sent a deadly email that pierced Don-aslan through the heart. The children rushed to help their noble entrepreneurial ally, but it was all in vain. The mighty magical celebrity business-lion was mortally wounded. He collapsed on the ninth hole of his magical golf

9

course and breathed his last. In the chaos, the Nasty Woman sleighed off again, with another evil, democratic cackle.

'All is lost!' exclaimed Steven Mnuchin, the talking gibbon, as everyone sobbed and mourned the death of their powerful and intelligent leader. Except that, the very next morning, Don-aslan surprisingly rose up from the dead, a bit like Jesus.

To the children, the magically resurrected Don-aslan's lustrous blond mane now seemed to be blonder and more lustrous than ever, and his facial fur glowed brighter orange than ever before.

'Now I'm not dead any more, it's time to defeat that crooked, Nasty Woman and lock her up!' said Don-aslan in a stirring and rousing speech to his supporters.

Fired up by the passion of the moment, Peter raised a sword above his head. 'To battle!' he cried. And so, the children went with Don-aslan and his supporters to face the Nasty Woman and her evil, democratic forces at the gates of the big white house. The two armies waged a terrible and vicious election campaign, which culminated in the ultimate battle of good against evil, as both sides took to the ballots and voted for their leader.

'I can count up the votes,' offered Lucy, quirkily. 'I'm good at counting!'

'I'll make us a nice cup of tea,' said Susan, sensibly.

But no matter how many times they counted the votes, it seemed there was no clear winner. They were about to call it a draw when, just then, Edmund stepped spitefully onto the battlefield.

'Wait,' he said. 'I haven't cast my vote yet,' he declared as his brother and sisters turned towards him.

'Oh, but you have to vote for Don-aslan,' pleaded Lucy. 'He's going to raise taxes on foreign imports to drive up Mel-narnian domestic industry and ban foreigners from entering the country.'

There was a very tense pause, while all the magical talking folk of Mel-narnia stared at Edmund.

'Well, I've decided,' said Edmund, 'that I am going to vote for Don-aslan. Partly because, even though I'm spiteful, I'm ultimately well-meaning. But also, because that Nasty Woman didn't give me any Turkish Delight, so I agree with the lion that she should be locked up.'

And that's how Don-aslan, the great, celebrity business-lion, became the fairest, most enlightened and modest ruler Mel-narnia had ever seen. Winter finally receded and Don-aslan spread the orange glow of spring across the land. Now that evil had been vanquished, the children returned to their wardrobe, where they lived happily ever after, while James McAvoy became the leader of the X-Men.

The End

45

DONALD "THE DONINATOR" TRUMP

CATCHPHRASE: "You're so, so, so, so weak!"

PHYSICAL STRENGTH:

NEMESIS: Kim "The Nuke" Jong-un

SIGNATURE MOVE: The Donald Thump

APOCALYPSE RATING:

WORLD WRESTLING PRESIDENTS

DONALD'S 'DONALD TRUMP YEARBOOK' EXPERT QUIZ

WE ALL LIKE TO THINK WE KNOW DONALD TRUMP VERY WELL, BUT HOW WELL DO YOU KNOW *THE DONALD TRUMP YEARBOOK*?

ANSWER THE QUESTIONS BELOW TO DISCOVER HOW MUCH OF A 'DONALD TRUMP YEARBOOK' EXPERT YOU REALLY ARE.

1. What is Jimmy Carter's Presidential SmackDown catchphrase?

- A) Eat my shorts
- B) Eat my nuts
- C) I've got a lovely bunch of coconuts

2. Which one of these options is a dessert from Donald's Diplomatic Dinner?

- A) A platter of American cheese
- B) Crème brûlée
- C) Rose-petal panna cotta with black chocolate shards

3. According to the rules of Trumpfulness you should 'build ------ not bridges'?

- A) Walls
- B) Friendships
- C) Furniture

4. What are Donald's naughty clones called?

- A) Munchkins
- B) Trumpkins
- C) Trumpalumpas

5. What type of aliens does Captain Trump of the Space Force defeat?

- ❏ A) Klingons
- ❏ B) Kimjongs
- ❏ C) Kim Cattrall

6. How many points do you get for a slam-putt-hole-in-one in Donald's Gasketbolf game?

- ❏ A) 13
- ❏ B) A birdie
- ❏ C) A doggie

7. Which of Donald's Hair Flair hairstyles represents the 1980s?

- ❏ A) The Flock of Seagulls
- ❏ B) The Flock of Seaweed
- ❏ C) The Flock of Sausages

8. What was one of the examples we gave you in The Language of Trump?

- ❏ A) Flagkefster
- ❏ B) Bleggnwf
- ❏ C) Mnmnmvgmcvxxx

9. Which 'Other President' does Bill Pullman play?

- ❏ A) Thomas J. Whitmore
- ❏ B) Michael J. Fox
- ❏ C) Donald J. Trump

10. What is the answer to question 10 in the 'Donald Trump Yearbook' expert quiz?

- ❏ A) ...
- ❏ B) 10?
- ❏ C) My brain hurts

Answers!

TRUMP CABANA TROPICAL BANANA WORD SEARCH

THE GREAT TRUMP CLONE HUNT GAME

Answers!

TEN-MINUTE TEATIME TRUMP-TEASER

```
                              S T O R M Y
                                      E
                                M     L
                              I V A N K A
                    P E N C E A R   A   N
                      L       P R E P U B L I C A N
                    U N I V E R S E   A   N
                      N       R   N   G
                    G O       E   T   O
                    O   Q     N   I   T O W E R
                  J O H N     T   C
                    F   U   Q U E E N S
                        E X E C U T I V E
                        E
                        N
                        S
```

DONALD'S 'DONALD TRUMP YEARBOOK' EXPERT QUIZ ANSWERS

1. B) Eat my nuts
2. A) A platter of American cheese
3. A) Walls
4. B) Trumpkins
5. B) Kimjongs

6. A) 13
7. A) The Flock of Seagulls
8. B) Bleggnwf
9. A) Thomas J. Whitmore
10. C) My brain hurts

PHOTO CREDITS